OFF-ROADING VEHICLES

UTVs

TAMRA B. ORR

I0795457

Mitchell Lane
PUBLISHERS

Parent and Caregiver Tips for Creating Nonfiction Readers

The high-interest topics in the *Off-Roading Vehicles* series are sure to get your young reader excited about reading nonfiction. While exploring a fascinating subject, your reader will be introduced to new concepts, facts, ideas, and vocabulary.

Tips for Reading Nonfiction

Talk about Nonfiction

Explain that nonfiction books provide facts about real-world topics. When readers read nonfiction, they gain a rich understanding of the world. They build background knowledge that provides a foundation for learning and academic success.

Look at the Parts

This book contains the following helpful features. Share the purpose of each feature with your reader.

Photos, Captions, and Graphic Aids
The photos, captions, charts, maps, and other graphic aids in nonfiction texts contain a wealth of information. Help your reader identify different ways information can be displayed. A special feature, "A Closer Look," puts the spotlight on learning through images.

Sidebars
These extra tidbits of information help satisfy readers' curiosity and expand their knowledge.

Table of Contents
Located at the front of the book, this list shows the big ideas within the text and the page numbers where they can be found.

Glossary
Located at the back of the book, the glossary defines key words and phrases that are related to the topic. These words and phrases can be found in the text in **bold** type.

Comprehension Questions (Fact Check)
Multiple-choice questions help readers self-check to make sure they understand what they read.

Index
Located at the back of the book, the index is an alphabetical list of topics and the page numbers where they can be found.

With a little help and guidance, your reader will be on their way to enjoying and learning from nonfiction books.

Mitchell Lane
PUBLISHERS
mitchelllanepub.com

2001 SW 31st Avenue
Hallandale, FL 33009

Copyright © 2026 by Mitchell Lane Publishers. All rights reserved. No part of this book may be reproduced without written permission from the publisher. Printed and bound in the United States of America.

First Edition, 2026.
Author: Tamra B. Orr
Designer: Kathy Walsh
Editor: Tricia Hoffman

Series: Off-Roading Vehicles
Title: UTVs / by Tamra B. Orr

Hallandale, FL : Mitchell Lane Publishers, [2026]

Library bound ISBN: 979-8-89260-568-7
Paperback ISBN: 979-8-89260-598-4
eBook ISBN: 979-8-89260-569-4

Photo Credits
Adobe: background, miloje; Alamy: p18 & 29, pierre rochon; p8, John Richmond; Dreamstine: Cover & Title pg, Kostya6969 Shutterstock: p21 & 29, Pukhov K; p10, 12 & 28, Anton Tolmachov; p17 & 29, Wirestock Creators; p6 & 28, Txgirl872; p5, Pukhov K; p7, Anton Tolmachov; p9, Aaron of L.A. Photography; p14, FS Stock; p15, Wieland Teixeira; p19, Tyson Curtis; p20, EvrenKalinbacak; p23, VD Image Lab; p25, adolf martinez doler; p26, Yaron's Drone Footage

Contents

Do it All

Do you need to haul hay from the barn?

Plow snow from the driveway?

Move sports equipment across the field?

Race over giant sand dunes?

Or rumble across rocky ground?

Then try a UTV!

Some people say that UTVs are the fastest-growing class of vehicles in all of off-roading. Why? Because these vehicles can do it all!

All Work and No Play?

UTV stands for utility task vehicle. It also stands for utility terrain vehicle. These versatile vehicles have many different names!

At first, UTVs were mainly meant to be **workhorses**. They were built to tow and carry heavy loads. UTVs were used on construction sites and on ranches. Their large engines, sturdy bodies, and plentiful storage room kept them always ready to tackle big jobs.

But then, people started taking an interest in off-roading adventures. And that's when the fun began!

BY ANY OTHER NAME

These vehicles are sometimes called Ultra-Terrain Vehicle, Unlimited Terrain Vehicle, and Recreational Off-Road Vehicle. The most popular name, however, is Side-by-Side or SXS.

Hard at Work

The Lockley Wrangler, produced in 1970, is considered by some to be the first ever UTV. It was an amphibious UTV, meaning it could go across both water and land. It could reach speeds of up to 50 miles (80.5 km) per hour.

But it wasn't until the next decade, when Kawasaki developed the MULE, that people really began to take notice.

In the 1980s, the MULE was built to be strong and durable. Its engine got bigger and more powerful, so it could handle tough work tasks with ease. It was small enough to squeeze through tight spaces, but didn't have much speed.

Kawasaki MULE

Yamaha YXZ1000R

GETTING POPULAR

Many different companies make UTVs today, but the most popular brands are Textron, Suzuki, Kawasaki, Honda, Yamaha, Can-Am, and Polaris.

The Fun Begins

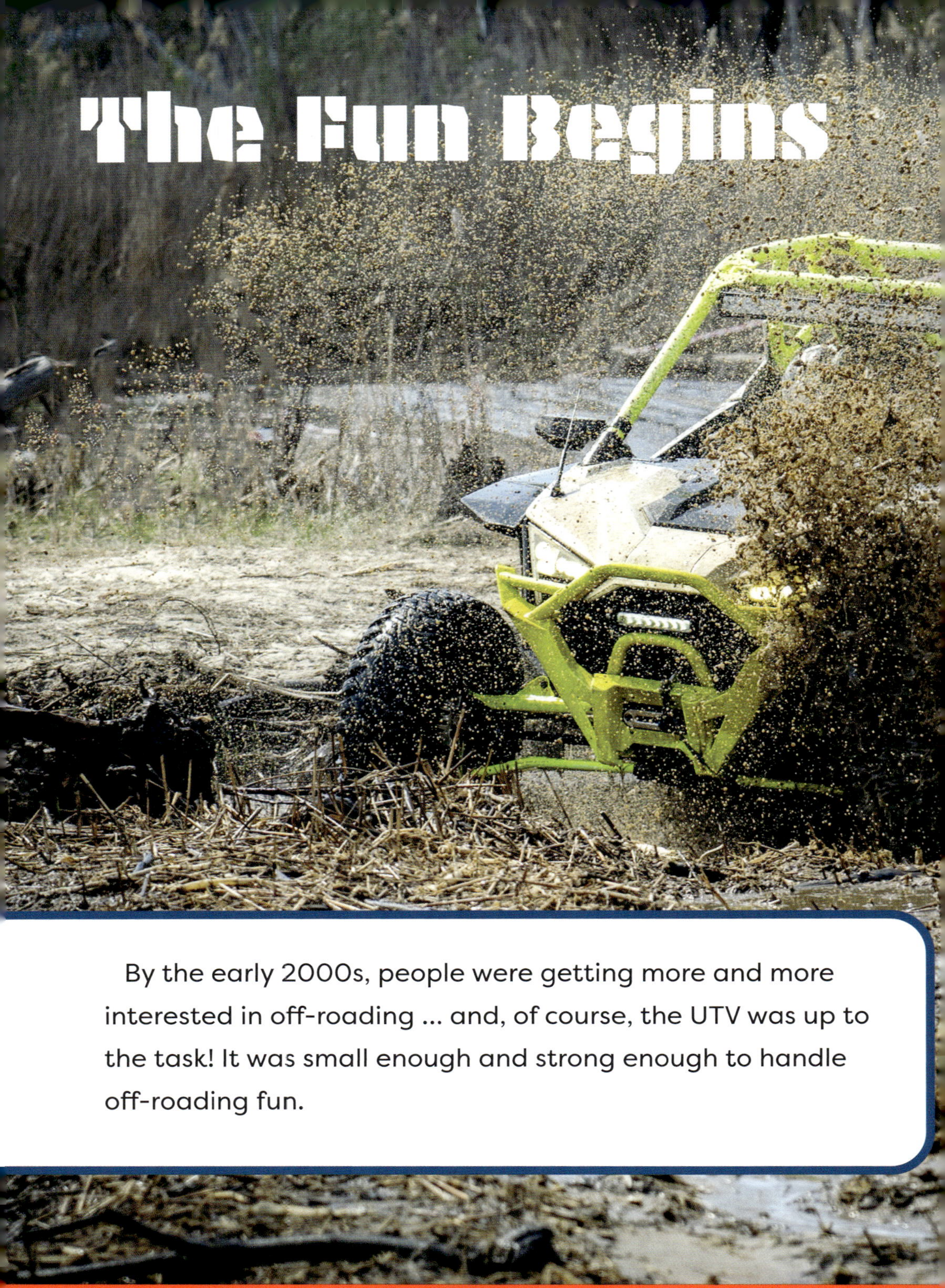

By the early 2000s, people were getting more and more interested in off-roading ... and, of course, the UTV was up to the task! It was small enough and strong enough to handle off-roading fun.

In 2007, Polaris manufactured the RZR. It was designed for speed, reaching up to 70 miles (112.7 km) per hour. It looked sporty and had a powerful engine. It could jump over and across rocky obstacles.

ALL ABOARD!

While most of today's UTVs seat two people, some models include room for two more. With the right **modifications**, up to six people can ride in one vehicle.

UTV vs. ATV... What's the Difference?

While it is easy to confuse the terms UTV with ATV (all-terrain vehicle), they are very different vehicles. ATVs are designed to be more like motorbikes. They have handlebars, can only carry one or two passengers, and are much smaller than UTVs.

ATVs can carry up to 400 pounds, which sounds like a lot. But UTVs can tote four times that amount! UTVs are designed to be more like cars, with regular seats, steering wheels, seat belts, and windshields.

Unlike an ATV's hand brakes and **throttle**, UTVs use two pedals to stop and go, just like cars do.

UTV owners often add modifications to their vehicles. For example, some add fog lights for better vision, or improve the overall suspension. Still others add a **dump bed** for hauling loads of dirt, or a **winch** for towing other vehicles.

Polaris Ranger

ALL YEAR LONG

In 2024, a new UTV was produced from the Massimo Group. Called the T-Boss, it has a fully enclosed cabin with a built-in heater to keep riders warm in the winter.

Safety First!

Just like any off-roading vehicle, the UTV has risks. Use caution while riding!

To help prevent injury, proper safety gear is a must. All riders should wear:

- √ helmets
- √ boots
- √ gloves
- √ long pants
- √ long-sleeved shirts
- √ goggles

And of course, riders should always fasten their seat belts!

HELMET UP

The best type of helmet to wear in a UTV is a full-face helmet that extends out in front of your mouth and chin.

Safety courses can be found online or in-person. They will include lessons on how to operate the vehicle, common **hazards**, and how to drive on hills, slippery surfaces, soft ground, and sand. They may also show drivers how to inspect their UTVs, perform basic **maintenance**, and safely load and transport the vehicle.

Some states allow UTVs to be driven on public streets, so owners need to check before heading down the road. If a UTV goes on public roads, it must have insurance and be registered—just like a car!

Polaris RZR

Time to Race

Once people started riding UTVs for fun, it wasn't long before races began popping up.

Some of these races were along dirt tracks. Others rolled through muddy, dense forests, while still others tackled towering sand dunes.

Sport UTVs were built for speed. They are great for fast races, but not the best choice for going over rough terrain.

Can-Am Maverick

UTVs used for racing must have safety equipment installed, including:

- √ **Roll cages:** a frame going around the vehicle's cabin to limit any damage done if the vehicle rolls over
- √ **Doors:** must lock so that they do not open during the race
- √ **Safety nets:** installed to prevent **debris** from flying into the UTV
- √ **Fire extinguisher:** vital in the rare case of fire
- √ **Harness:** 4- or 5-point for keeping passengers in their seats during a crash

RACING IN THE SAND

Hundreds of off-roading drivers have competed in the Dakar Rally, a race held in Saudi Arabia since 2020. Competitors race for two weeks across thousands of miles of sand.

To the Future

What will tomorrow's UTVs look like? They will be more environmentally friendly, thanks to the use of recyclable materials and fewer **emissions**.

Electric and hybrid UTVs have high-tech batteries that provide longer power and charge up quickly. Some UTVs will also be equipped with an advanced driver assistance system. This offers automatic braking and **collision detection**.

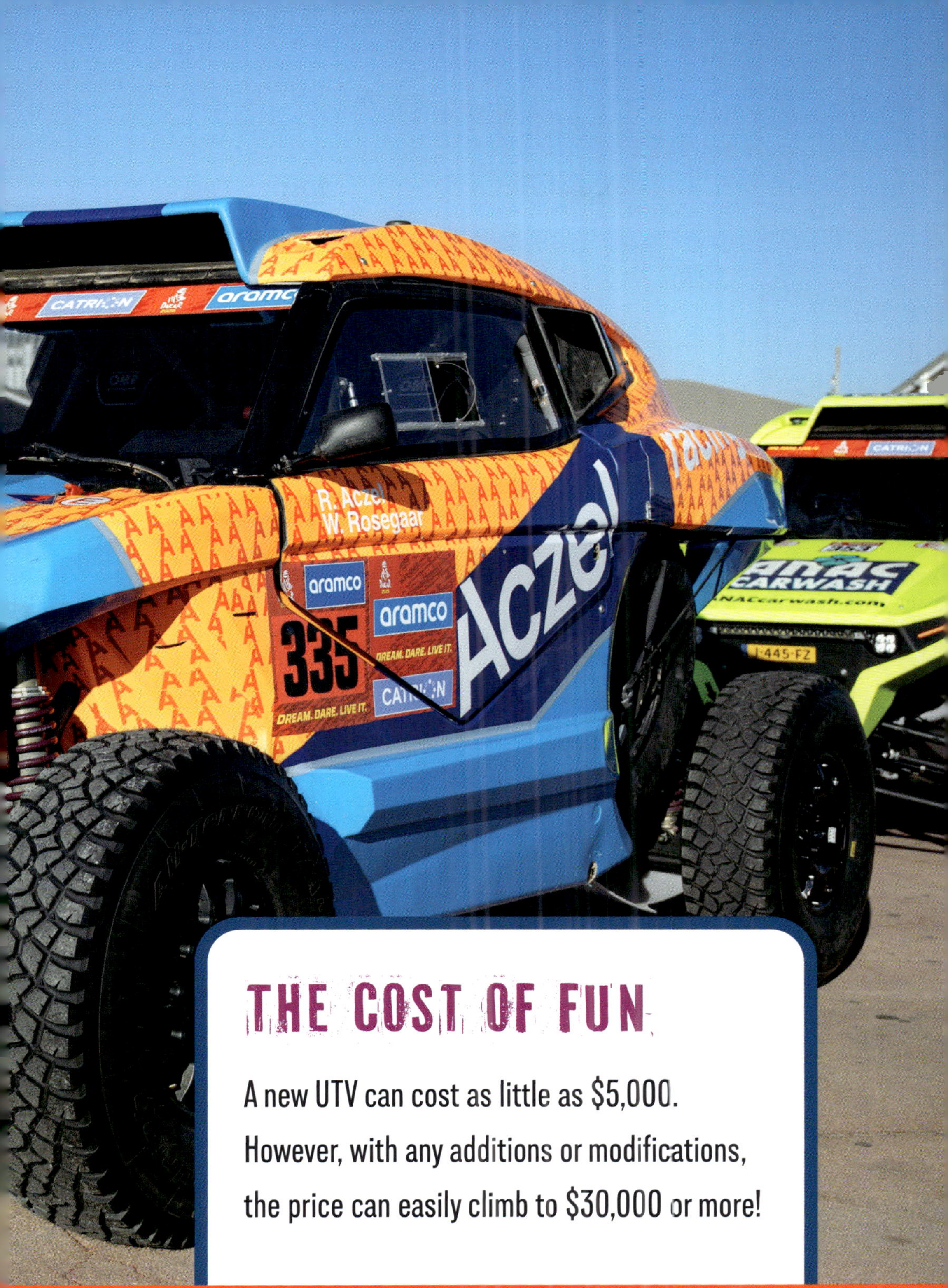

THE COST OF FUN

A new UTV can cost as little as $5,000. However, with any additions or modifications, the price can easily climb to $30,000 or more!

Climb On!

No matter what you need it for, a UTV is up for the job. These amazing vehicles really live up to the "utility tasks" part of their name!

Whether you're looking for a workhorse on the farm or an escape into nature, the UTV is ready, waiting, and more than able. So climb on, and see where the adventure takes you!

A Closer Look

Do farmers use UTVs?

Yes! UTVs are used to do lots of work on the farm. They may mow grass, plow snow, bring food to animals, carry firewood, move equipment from one field to another, and so much more!

Why is this UTV plowing through all that mud?

The driver is mud bogging! This means driving through deep mud pits or other muddy terrain. UTVs are perfect for this because of their small size and agility. Just be ready to be covered in mud!

Is that UTV winning a race against an ATV?

Looks like it! UTVs can go faster than ATVs. Plus, they tend to be safer for drivers and passengers.

Are helmets one-size-fits-all?

No. UTV riders should measure the circumference of their heads before purchasing a helmet. If a helmet is too big or too small, it won't provide the protection you need.

What is this UTV doing?

It's loaded onto a small trailer that's attached to the back of a truck. It isn't always possible to drive your UTV to its destination, so transporting it on a UTV trailer will allow you to take it to more places—and have more adventures!

Is this UTV flying?

No! But it is possible to jump a UTV, especially with enough speed over sand dunes. Their suspension systems can handle the impact of the landing without damaging the UTV.

Glossary

collision detection (kuh-LIZH-uhn di-TEK-shuhn)
a system using sensors to detect possible collisions and warn the driver

debris (duh-BREE)
remains of anything broken down; loose fragments of rock

dump bed (duhmp bed)
a UTV's truck bed that can tilt for easily unloading contents

emissions (i-MISH-uhnz)
gases released into the atmosphere as fuel is burned

hazards (HAZ-urdz)
dangers, or things that are likely to cause problems

maintenance (MAYN-tuh-nuhns)
the process of keeping something in good condition by checking and repairing it

modifications (mah-duh-fi-KAY-shuhnz)
altered or changed

throttle (THRAH-tuhl)
a piece of equipment that controls the amount of fuel that flows in a vehicle's engine

winch (winch)
a machine that lifts or pulls heavy objects; made up of cable wound around a rotating drum

workhorses (WURK-hors-ez)
people or machines that dependably perform hard work over a long time

Fact Check

1. Another popular name for UTVs is _____.
   A. ATV B. SXS C. RZR
2. As many as____ people can ride in a modified UTV.
   A. two B. four C. six
3. To keep passengers in their seats during a crash, racing UTVs must have a _____.
   A. safety net B. fire extinguisher C. harness
4. All racing UTVs must have _____ installed.
   A. roll cages B. collision detection systems C. fog lights

Answers: 1. B, 2. C, 3. C, 4. A

Further Reading

David, Jack. *ATVs (Torque: Cool Rides)*. Childrens Press, 2008.

Landers, Ace. *Hot Wheels Off-Roading*. Scholastic, 2008.

Peppas, Lynn. *ATVs and Off-Roaders*. Crabtree Publishing, 2012.

Worms, Penny. *Off-Road Vehicles*. Smart Apple Media, 2016.

Zobel, Derek. *Monster Vehicles*. Bellwether Media, 2008.

On the Internet

Dakar Rally
www.dakar.com/en
Check out the latest updates, results, and highlights from the Dakar Rally in Saudi Arabia

The Evolution of UTVs: From Workhorses to Adventure Machines
revolutionor.com/blogs/utv-tech-tips/the-evolution-of-utvs-from-workhorses-to-adventure-machines
Learn more about the history of UTVs, from their beginnings to today.

What is UTV Racing?
www.redbull.com/us-en/utv-racing-guide
Read all about the different types of UTV racing across the globe.

Index

About the Author

Tamra B. Orr is a mom, wife, grandmother, and full-time writer and author living in the beautiful all-terrain Pacific Northwest. She lives in Oregon, a state that offers UTV riders 3,840 square acres of dunes. The area features everything from towering sand dunes to thick forests to sparkling ocean. A graduate of Ball State University, she has written more than 750 nonfiction and educational books for readers of all ages and loves her job. It gives her the chance to learn about something new—and then share that information—every single day.